What Pilots Need to Know

Diane Lindsey Reeves

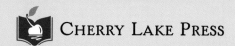

CHERRY LAKE PRESS

Published in the United States of America by Cherry Lake Publishing Group
Ann Arbor, Michigan
www.cherrylakepublishing.com

Reading Adviser: Beth Walker Gambro, MS, Ed., Reading Consultant, Yorkville, IL

Photo Credits: © DC Studio/Shutterstock, cover, 1; San Diego Air & Space Museum Archives, No restrictions, via Wikimedia Commons, 5; © Andrei Armiagov/Shutterstock, 7; © Miguel Lagoa/Shutterstock, 8; George Grantham Bain Collection, Public domain, via Wikimedia Commons, 9; © Olena Yakobchuk/Shutterstock, 11; © FTiare/Shutterstock, 13; © LightField Studios/Shutterstock, 15; © Mario Hagen/Shutterstock, 16; © Pete Pahham/Shutterstock, 18; © kelvn/Shutterstock, 19; SDASM Archives, Public domain, via Wikimedia Commons, 21; © Goran Jakus/Shutterstock, 22; © M-Production/Shutterstock, 23; © EmiliaUngur/Shutterstock, 25; © Randy Miramontez/Shutterstock, 26; © Orientaly/Shutterstock, 28; © Alisha Falcone/Shutterstock, 29

Cherry Lake Press is an imprint of Cherry Lake Publishing Group.

Library of Congress Cataloging-in-Publication Data has been filed and is available at catalog.loc.gov.

Cherry Lake Publishing Group would like to acknowledge the work of the Partnership for 21st Century Learning, a Network of Battelle for Kids. Please visit Battelle for Kids online for more information.

Printed in the United States of America

Note from publisher: Websites change regularly, and their future contents are outside of our control. Supervise children when conducting any recommended online searches for extended learning opportunities.

Diane Lindsey Reeves likes to write books that help students figure out what they want to be when they grow up. She mostly lives in Washington, D.C., but spends as much time as she can in North Carolina and South Carolina with her grandkids.

CONTENTS

In the Know

Every career you can imagine has one thing in common. It takes an expert. Career experts need to know more about how to do a specific job than other people do. That is how everyone from plumbers to rocket scientists gets their job done.

Sometimes it takes years of college study to learn what they need to know. Other times, people learn by working alongside someone who is already a career expert. No matter how they learn, it takes a career expert to do any job well.

Take pilots, for instance. They need to know how to fly amazing aircraft. They need to know how to **navigate** from one place to another. They need to understand physics. They need solid math skills.

What about you? Can you see yourself in the **cockpit** of an airplane someday? Here are some things future pilots need to know.

Famous Firsts

Charles Lindbergh was the first man to fly alone across the Atlantic Ocean. He flew from New York to Paris in May 1927. The flight took more than 33 hours.

In 1928, Amelia Earhart was the first woman to fly solo across the Atlantic. She was also the first person to fly across both the Atlantic and the Pacific Oceans. She was trying to be the first to fly around the world when she disappeared over the Pacific in 1937. Her body was never found.

CHAPTER 1

Pilots Know... How Airplanes Fly

The idea of flight might seem like a wonderful mystery. How in the world do planes full of people and cargo fly like birds in the sky?

Aerodynamics explains how it happens. There are four forces at work when an airplane flies. These forces are **lift**, **weight**, **thrust**, and **drag**. Each force works in an opposite direction.

For instance, lift moves the plane upward. It is created by airplane wings. Wings push the air down, and air pushes the wings up.

There are three main kinds of airplanes that fly across the world: passenger planes, cargo planes, and military planes.

When we fly on airplanes, we are hardly even aware of the forces at play keeping the plane balanced in the sky. These forces (lift, thrust, drag, and weight) keep the aircraft flying along!

Weight is a downward force. Any object on Earth is pulled down by gravity. When the plane's weight is balanced, the plane stays balanced. Too much weight in the nose or tail of a plane would cause it to tip.

Thrust moves the plane forward. Thrust happens when air is pulled in and pushed out in the opposite direction. Propellers, jet engines, and rockets create thrust in aircraft.

Drag, or wind resistance, acts against thrust. It slows down the plane with a backward-acting force. Drag is like trying to walk against a heavy wind. The shape of an aircraft is one of several things that affect drag.

Airplanes fly when all four of these forces work together. It is proof of an important law of physics. It is Sir Isaac Newton's third law of motion. He discovered it in 1686. It says that "for every action, there is an equal, but opposite, action." This solves the mystery of flight. And it's the first thing pilots need to know.

FLYING INTO HISTORY

The Wright brothers, Orville and Wilbur, invented the first powered airplane. On December 17, 1903, they made the first successful flight. That first flight lasted only 12 seconds. But it forever changed the way people travel. It's a fascinating story of innovation and persistence. Ask an adult to help you find out more about it in books and online.

CHAPTER 2

Pilots Know... How to Earn Their Wings

You aren't a pilot until the Federal Aviation Administration (FAA) says you're a pilot. The FAA doesn't say you are a pilot until you get a license. Earning a license involves lots of time flying. It also means passing lots of tests.

The type of license you need depends on the type of aircraft you want to fly. There are different rules for airplanes and helicopters. There are even rules about getting a license to fly a glider or hot-air balloon!

It starts with a student license. You can apply for this license if you are at least 16 years old. You have to pass a medical exam to qualify. You can start learning before you get this license. However, you cannot fly solo until you get it.

It's estimated that there are roughly between 1.5 and 2.3 million pilots across the globe, including about 735,000 just in the United States alone.

Other types of licenses include those for recreational pilots, private pilots, commercial pilots, and airline transport pilots. All require training and lots of flying. Each type of license has rules about the kinds of passengers and cargo you can have on board when you fly.

There is so much to learn about flying. Pilots learn a lot about different aircraft. They pay attention to the weather so they can plan safe flights. They know how to use all the instruments in the cockpit. They can navigate from one place to another. They know how to communicate with **air traffic control**.

EYE ON THE SKY

Many types of aircraft take to the skies every day. Can you tell the difference between an Airbus A380 and a Boeing 747? Ask a trusted adult to help you find a local plane-spotting location. Plane spotting is a hobby for people who enjoy watching planes take off and land. With practice, you can learn to identify many types of planes. You can also go online with the help of a trusted adult and find out all you can about different types of planes. Keep a log of all your discoveries.

Pilots use special weather detection technology on their aircraft to determine if thunderstorms are safe to fly through!

All pilots also learn how to respond to "what if" situations. What if the weather takes a turn for the worse? What if the plane's engine fails? What if a passenger has a heart attack? Pilots must be ready to act quickly in an emergency.

The stakes are high for pilots. They must make smart decisions while flying at fast speeds at high altitudes.

CHAPTER 3

Pilots Know... How Cockpits Work

Look into the cockpit of an airplane and one thing is clear. There is a lot going on in there! There is row after row of gadgets and gauges. Each one has a special job to do.

Six of these instruments are especially important. You find them in airplanes of all sizes. They are known as the six pack. The six pack includes the airspeed indicator, attitude indicator, and altimeter. It also includes the vertical speed indicator, heading indicator, and turn coordinator.

The airspeed indicator works like a speedometer in a car. It shows how fast the plane is moving through the air.

At first glance, cockpits of airplanes can seem like very complicated places, but pilots study very hard to understand each device and its purpose.

Pilots practice using radar control and navigation panels in flight simulators to get comfortable with the complicated machinery.

The attitude indicator is also known as the artificial horizon. It is a gyroscope that lets pilots know if the plane is straight and level.

The altimeter is one of the most important instruments. It measures the height of the aircraft. It tells the pilot how high above sea level the plane is flying.

The vertical speed indicator is similar to the airspeed indicator. Its job is to show the pilot the rate of speed when climbing or descending.

The heading indicator is a magnetic compass. It shows which direction the airplane is traveling. It helps pilots stay on course.

A turn coordinator does exactly what its name suggests. It helps pilots coordinate turns. It warns pilots if the plane is slipping or skidding.

There are many other instruments in the cockpit. All are within easy reach of the cockpit crew. They have everything they need to communicate with air traffic control. They have monitors that let them know that vital systems like

CAN YOU SPEAK PILOT?

Pilots use all kinds of special terms to communicate clearly with air traffic control—or ATC, as they would say. They even have their own alphabet. It starts with *alpha* and ends with *Zulu*. Go online to look for "aviation alphabet," "pilot's alphabet," or "International Civil Aviation Organization (ICAO) phonetic alphabet." A trusted adult can help you practice pilot talk.

During takeoff and landing, pilots communicate with air traffic control to make sure runways are clear and conditions are safe.

During the flight, air cabin crews have the important job of taking care of passengers.

engines and brakes are working correctly. The yoke is what pilots use to steer a plane. The throttle is how they adjust engine power.

Takeoff and landing keep pilots especially busy. Once a plane takes off, pilots often put the plane on autopilot. These high-tech systems keep planes on track without hands-on help from pilots.

CHAPTER 4

Pilots Know... How to Fly Safely

The first thing pilots do to keep air travel safe is take good care of themselves. They must pass medical exams every 6 months to 5 years in order to fly. Good eyesight and hearing are musts. Illegal drug use and substance abuse are absolute no-nos. Certain medical conditions like heart issues disqualify pilots from flying.

Big problems can happen if a pilot has a medical problem while flying. That is one reason why commercial flights require at least two pilots in the cockpit at all times. If something happens to one of them, the other pilot can take over.

Helen Richey became the first female pilot to fly a commercial passenger aircraft on December 31, 1934, with Central Airlines.

Everything pilots do once they enter the cockpit for a flight is about safety. They use a preflight checklist to make sure everything is as it should be. Their goal is to make sure that all systems are airworthy. This includes everything from fuel and oil levels to the landing gear and flight plan.

Once passengers board a plane, there are even more safety concerns. Seat belts are a big deal. The pilot makes sure everyone uses them for takeoff and landing. They also turn on seat belt warnings when the plane encounters rough patches of air.

There are rules about passenger behavior. As the boss of the flight, pilots must enforce the rules.

TRUE OR FALSE

It is safer to travel in a car than it is to fly in an airplane.

Answer: False. A person's chances of being killed in a plane crash are 1 in 11 million. The average person has a 1 in 5,000 chance of being killed in a car accident. Bottom line? Stay safe out there!

The "fasten seat belt" signal lights up when there is turbulence.
Pilots want to keep passengers safe!

Pilots stay alert to weather changes during a flight.
Sometimes they need to adjust the plane's altitude
to avoid **turbulence**. Other times, a pilot may need
to adjust the flight plan or change the plane's route.

The chance of accidents increases during takeoff and
landing. Pilots depend on instructions from air traffic
controllers to keep everyone safe. That's how they avoid
hitting other aircraft. It's also how they know which
runways to use.

Keeping people and property safe is what pilots do best.
That's what everything they do before, during, and after
a flight is all about.

CHAPTER 5

Pilots Know... How to Find the Job They Want

Once you earn your pilot's license, there are quite a few ways you can take to the skies. Many pilots get their start as military pilots. That's where they get top-notch training. They also get experience flying different types of aircraft. From there, the sky is the limit as to where they want to take their careers.

The most elite military pilots fly fighter jets in combat situations. These jets cost many millions of dollars. Only the very best pilots are trusted to fly them.

Compared to commercial airlines, fighter jets typically can only carry one or two people, and both can usually pilot the aircraft.

Other military pilots fly cargo planes that move people and cargo from one place to another. Military helicopters are mostly used to transport troops. They can be used in combat search and rescue missions. They are also used to transport wounded troops to medical facilities. This is called medical evacuation.

Commercial pilots fly airplanes that carry human passengers. Some fly small commuter planes that carry up to 100 people. Big commercial jets can carry several hundred people. Commercial pilots fly different types of routes.

A CLAIM TO FAME

Chuck Yeager is one of the most famous test pilots ever known. Among other great feats, he was the first pilot in history to go faster than the speed of sound. This was back in October 1947 and was followed by other record-breaking flights. Ask an adult to help you find online resources about this flying ace.

FedEx has the world's largest cargo air fleet with more than 650 planes.

International pilots fly from one country to another. Domestic pilots fly planes within one country. Regional pilots fly shorter distances. They may fly from one city to another in the same state. Or they may fly between states in a specific part of the country.

Cargo pilots fly mail and other goods for the U.S. Postal Service, FedEx, UPS, and other cargo companies. They may fly short distances or cover long-haul flights overseas.

Crop duster planes cost roughly $1 million and can cost up to $2 million depending on the model.

Agricultural pilots work in areas rich in farmland like Iowa and Kansas. Their small planes are called crop dusters. They use them to water or fertilize crops in large commercial fields.

Government pilots work for agencies like the FBI, Homeland Security, and police departments. They may fly helicopters or small jets. These aircraft are used to get government personnel where they are needed most.

Corporate or private pilots fly businesspeople and others who can afford this luxury. They take these people wherever they want to go.

Firefighter pilots are among the most daring pilots of all. They fight out-of-control wildfires. Their work saves lives, property, and woodlands.

Flight instructors are experienced pilots who teach other pilots how to fly. They often specialize in a certain type of aircraft. Their classes take place on land and in the sky.

Test pilots are experienced pilots who try out new types of aircraft. They work closely with engineers and flight crews. Their job is to identify problems with technology and other equipment.

Activity

Stop, Think, and Write

It's not like just anyone can fly an airplane. Can you imagine a world without pilots?

Get a separate sheet of paper. On one side, answer these questions:

- *How do pilots make the world a better place?*
- *If you were a pilot, what kind would you want to be?*
- *Where would you like to go?*

On the other side of the paper:

- *Draw a picture of you taking off into the wild blue yonder!*

Things to Do If You Want to Be a Pilot

As many as 50 percent of today's qualified pilots are expected to retire in the next 15 years. That means there will be a great demand for new pilots. Here are some ideas to find out more about this career path.

NOW

- Ask an adult to help you check out programs offered by the Experimental Aircraft Association (EAA). They offer aviation clubs and camps for kids.

- Put together a model airplane to get a better idea of how airplanes are made.

- Visit airports and watch all the action.

- Learn all you can about airplanes and the history of flight.

LATER

- Earn your high school diploma.

- Pilots are not required to have a college degree. However, many big airlines prefer to hire those who do.

- Go to flight school and earn your pilot's license.

- Consider joining the military to get flight training and experience. Several branches of the military train pilots.

Learn More

Books

Grant, R. G. *Flight: Riveting Reads for Kids.* New York, NY: DK Publishing, 2020.

Kelley, Justin. *Ask a Pilot: A Pilot Answers Kids' Top Questions About Flying.* Fresno, CA: Bushel & Peck, 2021.

Rhatigan, Joe. *Get a Job: At the Airport.* Ann Arbor, MI: Cherry Lake, 2016.

On the Web

With an adult, learn more online with these suggested searches.

Boeing Future of Flight

Orville and Wilbur Wright

Smithsonian National Air and Space Museum

The History of Flight

Glossary

aerodynamics (air-oh-diye-NAM-iks) qualities of an object that affect how it moves through air

air traffic control (AIR TRAf-ik kuhn-TROHL) a group of experts on the ground who monitor and direct the movements of aircraft

altitudes (AL-tuh-toodz) heights of things above the ground or sea level

cockpit (KAHK-pit) the area in the front of the plane where a pilot controls an aircraft

drag (DRAG) the force that resists movement of an aircraft through the air; it is the opposite of thrust

lift (LIFT) the force that helps an airplane offset its weight so it can rise into the air and maintain altitude

navigate (NAV-uh-gayt) to operate or control the course of travel

thrust (THRUHST) a powerful force produced by an engine or propeller that moves an airplane forward; it is the opposite of drag

turbulence (TUHR-byuh-luhns) strong sudden movements within air or water

weight (WAYT) the force with which gravity pushes a body toward the center of Earth

Index